D0768822

Be a Maker!

Maker Projects for Kids Who Love

DESIGNING SPACES

MEGAN KOPP

Crabtree Publishing Company

www.crabtreebooks.com

Crabtree Publishing Company

www.crabtreebooks.com

Author: Megan Kopp

Series Research and Development: Reagan Miller

Editors: Sarah Eason, Harriet McGregor,
Tim Cooke, and Philip Gebhardt

Proofreaders: Claudia Martin, Wendy Scavuzzo,
and Petrice Custance

Editorial director: Kathy Middleton

Design: Paul Myerscough

Cover design: Paul Myerscough

Photo research: Rachel Blount

**Production coordinator and
Prepress technician:** Tammy McGarr

Print coordinator: Katherine Berti

Consultant: Jennifer Turliuk, Bachelor of Commerce,
Singularity University Graduate Studies Program at NASA
Ames, Former President of MakerKids

Production coordinated by Calcium Creative

Photo Credits:

t=Top, bl=Bottom Left, br=Bottom Right

www.cubeproject.org.uk: Theo Cohen: pp. 1, 15; o+a.com: Jasper Sanidad:
pp. 6, 11; Shutterstock: Baloncici: 27; Bikeriderlondon: p. 8; Cate_89: p. 23;
LI CHAOSHU: p. 10, Envyligh: p. 17; Gorin: p. 22; MR. INTERIOR: p. 26;
Momopixs: p. 16; Monkey Business Images: p. 5; Photographee.eu: p. 4;
PlusONE: pp. 9, 24; Sedat Seven: p. 14; Iriana Shiyan: p. 25; Tsyhun: p. 18;
Zastolskiy Victor: p. 19; Stanford d.school: p. 7; Tudor Photography:
pp. 12–13, 20–21, 28–29.

Cover: Tudor Photography

Library and Archives Canada Cataloguing in Publication

Kopp, Megan, author
    Maker projects for kids who love designing spaces /
Megan Kopp.

(Be a maker!)
Includes index.
Issued in print and electronic formats.
ISBN 978-0-7787-2574-9 (hardback).--
ISBN 978-0-7787-2580-0 (paperback).--
ISBN 978-1-4271-1762-5 (html)

    1. Interior design--Juvenile literature. 2. Handicraft--
Juvenile literature. I. Title.

NK2110.K66 2016   j747   C2016-903323-6
                                       C2016-903324-4

Library of Congress Cataloging-in-Publication Data

Names: Kopp, Megan, author.
Title: Maker projects for kids who love designing spaces /
Megan Kopp.
Description: New York : Crabtree Publishing, 2017. |
Series: Be a maker! | Includes index.
Identifiers: LCCN 2016026028 (print) | LCCN 2016026277 (ebook)
ISBN 9780778725749 (reinforced library binding) |
ISBN 9780778725800 (pbk.) |
ISBN 9781427117625 (Electronic HTML)
Subjects: LCSH: Handicraft--Juvenile literature. | Interior
  decoration--Juvenile literature.
Classification: LCC TT160 .K66 2016 (print) | LCC TT160 (ebook)
| DDC 745.5--dc23
LC record available at https://lccn.loc.gov/2016026028

Crabtree Publishing Company

www.crabtreebooks.com   1-800-387-7650

Printed in Canada/072016/EF20160630

**Published in Canada
Crabtree Publishing**
616 Welland Ave.
St. Catharines, Ontario
L2M 5V6

**Published in the United States
Crabtree Publishing**
PMB 59051
350 Fifth Avenue, 59th Floor
New York, New York 10118

**Published in the United Kingdom
Crabtree Publishing**
Maritime House
Basin Road North, Hove
BN41 1WR

**Published in Australia
Crabtree Publishing**
3 Charles Street
Coburg North
VIC, 3058

CONTENTS

TIME TO DESIGN

What revolves around space, can sometimes be dull, and is often overlooked? Interior design. It is all around us. Fast-food restaurants, hotel rooms, and even your dentist's office rely on **interior designers** to create a sense of space. Some interior designers work on stores, restaurants, and other business spaces. Others work on homes. Interior designers are makers. Makers take chances. They risk failure to find innovative solutions to problems. They keep trying until they succeed.

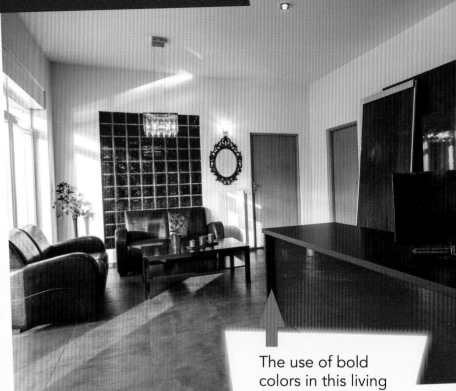

The use of bold colors in this living room design give it a dynamic and dramatic feel.

MAKING A MOVE

The maker movement is all about learning through hands-on, real-world experience. Designing spaces is part of the maker movement. A place where people can gather to share resources and knowledge, and work on projects is called a **makerspace**. The result of **collaborative** workspaces is a sharing of ideas. It is a future in which technology blends with other skills.

FUTURE IS PRESENT

IDEO is a maker community based in California's Silicon Valley, but has offices around the world. They are, in their own words, a collection of "makers, designers, hackers, builders, thinkers, explorers, writers, listeners, risk-takers, and doers." They design products and spaces and many other things. One of their tasks was to envision a future kitchen. A highlight from the design was a table that recognizes food set down on it and suggests recipes suited to the food and the amount of time you have available—the table even has a built-in cooking surface. Design heats up when brilliant minds work together with technology!

Interior designers need creativity, of course! They also need background knowledge, math skills, and the ability to communicate well with others. Read on, and get ready to make your mark on designing spaces!

Collaboration, or working as a team, is a very important aspect of the maker movement. Team work enhances creativity!

Be a Maker!

This book is like a mini-makerspace. It gives you some of the knowledge required by interior designers. It provides a creative springboard for your own designs. It allows you to think critically about design and how it impacts our lives.

MORE THAN A PLACE

Interior design is the way a space looks, feels, and works. What was the first example of interior design? Some people look as far back as cave paintings. This artwork changes the look of the space, even though it was not drawn for that reason. In the Middle Ages, most spaces were designed for **function** rather than appearance.

INDUSTRIAL AGE

A couple of **centuries** later, the rise of industry meant factories could make affordable decorative objects. Makers took design and made it less about purpose and more about appearance. In the 1800s, homes were full of flowery patterns, pretty but useless knickknacks, and uncomfortable, overstuffed furniture.

CREATIVE, COLORFUL, AND FUN!

Modern design is stylish with a trend of using less. Spaces are colorful, but still light and airy. Interiors are designed for people and purpose. Reality TV shows have made the design process a little easier to understand. Large companies are taking interior design to work.

This workplace has been designed with cool "pods" where workers can read or meet to share ideas.

Creative design in educational spaces, such as schools, can create a sense of fun and adventure, which encourages children to explore and learn.

Be a Maker!

The purpose of a space and how it will be used is important in design. At Stanford University, d.school (where students study design) has rooms with chairs that are uncomfortable. Why? It keeps meetings short and encourages people to stand while they interact, which helps improve creativity. Think about a space in your school. What is its purpose? How would you redesign that space so that it is used more effectively?

The offices of movie company Pixar were redesigned to pull the entire team together into one big office instead of three separate buildings. It encourages creative flow and casual connections between computer scientists, the artists who bring the characters to life on screen, the people who manage the business, and the editors. Swatch—the Swiss watch company—uses color and modern design to spice up its space.

GOOGLE IT!

Google's New York City office is also designed to encourage collaboration and creativity. Vertical ladders and a slide allow for fun and casual conversation as workers travel between floors instead of waiting for slow elevators. Two small meeting rooms are designed to look like cluttered studio apartments. One of the rooms has sofas made from bathtubs with a side sliced off. In the library, large wing-backed chairs use a wool suit as **upholstery** and have neckties sewn onto the backrests.

BACK TO BASICS

Interior design is about creativity. It is expressed in color, form, and line. Designing spaces requires an understanding of **scale** and **proportion**. It is both an art and a science.

ELEMENTS

Design involves five basic **elements**:

- *Color*—important for creating a feeling in a room
- *Form*—the overall shape of an object
- *Line*—horizontal, vertical, or curving directions created by furniture and the space's design
- *Pattern*—forms arranged in an organized manner
- **Texture**—the physical feel or surface appearance of a piece of furniture, a wall, or a window treatment

COMPOSING THE PICTURE

All designers use these elements to achieve certain effects. These elements need to work together in a complete design. How they are combined is called **composition**. Composition includes seven basic design values:

- **Unity**—an overall sense of belonging together
- **Harmony**—the blending of similar elements
- *Rhythm*—an easy flow as your eyes move around the room

Compare the design of this workspace with the one opposite. Which would you prefer to work in? Why?

8

- *Emphasis*—also called a focal point, a place that immediately draws the viewer's eye
- *Scale*—the overall size of a piece
- *Balance*—a sense of **symmetry** and evenness in the placement of objects
- *Function*—how a space works for its intended use

DO IT ONCE, DO IT RIGHT!

Good designs are obvious. They spark positive responses. They appeal in ways you do not even realize, and they feel restful. Poor designs feel awkward and unplanned. Sometimes there is too much happening and the space feels **chaotic**. Interior designers understand how color, lighting, room size, scale, and the arrangement of furniture and **accessories** all affect how items look in a room.

This workspace is designed with balance and harmony. It is a calm, inviting place in which to work.

Makers and Shakers

Sam Perry Allen

Most kids would not pretend to be sick so they could skip school and follow their mother—an interior designer—to meet **clients**. But Sam Perry Allen (born 1992) was not like most kids. At 12, Sam was helping out at a high-end home store in Westport, Connecticut. Five years later, he had his first **commission** turning a nanny suite into a playroom complete with a candy station and a hot-pink mini-fridge. By initially charging less than other designers and posting photos of his work on Facebook, Sam built up a client list. At 23, he now runs his own high-end design company.

COLOR ME HAPPY

Color, pattern, and texture are important elements for creating style. They are the building blocks of an interior design **palette**. Think of the Google company colors—blue, red, yellow, and green. These brilliant colors are used on the walls, furniture, and flooring in their office designs to create a fun and interesting workspace.

AT THE END OF THE RAINBOW

Color is a powerful design element. Color can change your mood and affect how you look at a space. Have you ever thought about painting your bedroom? According to one study, if teens could change one aspect of their room, 46 percent would paint it a new color.

Rooms can be made to look bigger by using light, cool colors. Big spaces can handle darker, warm colors. Ceilings look higher when painted with a light color, and lower when painted dark. Choose a **neutral color** for the majority of your painted surfaces and save splashes of strong colors for small feature spaces.

The use of white gives a space a light, airy feel. This area feels open and spacious because of its light colors.

PEEKING AT PATTERNS

Patterns have personality. There are bold **geometric** designs, playful checks, and graceful **floral** patterns. Knowing how to use patterns effectively can be a little confusing. It is a skill that takes time to develop. Start slow and use up to three different patterns that have similar colors. Be sure to look at their size in relation to each other and the space. Patterns can quickly overwhelm a room. Done correctly, patterns on area rugs, furniture, drapes, or within artwork on the walls can bring a space to life.

THE TRUTH ABOUT TEXTURE

Rough wooden ceiling beams, a stone fireplace, and a chunky throw on the couch—imagine this kind of space, and you are thinking of how a designer might create a simple, country theme. Each of these elements adds texture to the space. So do glass, metal, silk, and tile. Texture is all about touch and feel. Neutral rooms use texture to help make them visually interesting.

The bold geometric designs and bright colors used in this space give it a very cool contemporary, or modern, feel.

Be a Maker!

Looking at a design with a critical eye does not mean criticizing everything. It means thoughtful consideration of what works and what does not work and how it could be improved. Pick a room in your home and look at it critically. What works and what does not work? How could you fix it if budget, or the amount of money you have to spend, was not an issue?

MAKE IT!
IDEAS BOARD

One of the tools interior designers use for their projects is an ideas board. It is simply a collection of fabric samples, color choices, and cut-out magazine photos of furniture or artwork for inspiration. Putting them together gives you a visual of how these design elements work with one another. Work with your friends as a team to create an ideas board that you all love.

YOU WILL NEED
- Foam board or cardboard
- Fabric, wallpaper, and paint swatches; ribbons; magazine pictures; anything that says you!
- Glue
- Paperclips
- Push pins
- Scissors
- Pinking shears

1
- Find a board to work on.
- Collect samples. If you see something in a magazine, cut it out and save it in a file. Take digital pictures of rooms or designs you see and like.

2
- Cut or trim your images. Pinking shears give a professional look.

- Arrange everything on your board, looking at color, pattern, and texture.
- Pin, stick, or clip everything in place.
- You can add or remove items. You can replace an item with something else. You can move items around the board.

3

CONCLUSION

Look at your finished ideas board. Does it pull together all the themes you want to use in your room design? Do the colors, textures, and patterns work well together? Talk with your friends. What works well? What could you change to improve your board?

Make It Even Better!

What worked well on your ideas board? Why do you think it works? Discuss as a team if there is anything that you could change to make the design stronger. Pick another room and build a design board for it that works well with the first design, but differs in fabric choices and inspirational photos.

FINDING THE FOCUS

Walk into a cluttered room without a focal point and you will not know where to look. In a well-designed room, your eyes always return to the focal point of the space. It could be a fireplace, a big window, a built-in desk, or a large mirror or artwork on a wall. Sometimes focal points are obvious—like a fireplace. There are other times when you need to create a focal point. This can be done by painting a wall, hanging a large piece of art, or placing a striking piece of furniture, so your eyes are drawn to it.

The large, striking clock in this room is its focal feature. It draws your eye directly toward it.

14

DESIGN WITH FOCUS

Once you have picked out a focal point for your design, you can start to decorate around it. Artwork can be framed with chairs on either side. Pick a color from the focal point and use it in other items in the room, such as the rugs, curtains, or furniture. The focal point helps balance the room. Sometimes the focal point is blocked by furniture. Decide how to rearrange the furniture to open up the space and allow the focal point to shine.

The red of the blanket on the bed (the focal point in this space) is reflected throughout the space. This ties the design together—notice the red toaster and kettle.

Be a Maker!

Tiny homes are gaining ground. Lots of people are choosing the freedom of living in a small space instead of choosing an elaborate design. Many of these homes have an area that is smaller than a single bedroom in a larger home. Finding ways to use small spaces creatively is a brilliant challenge for makers. Check out the Lego-style apartment or Cube home video on YouTube. Could you see yourself living in a space this small one day? What changes, if any, would you make to these designs? Work with a friend or a family member to design a floor plan for a tiny bedroom for each other. Consider each other's personality and needs as you put together your designs.

A FINE BALANCE

Palaces used to be hard to furnish. The scale of the individual pieces needed to be huge to fit into the space. Today's mansions have the same issue and designers work creatively to make the space functional and beautiful.

SCALE

Most of us do not live in gigantic homes. Still, the scale of individual elements in a space and how the sizes of all the pieces compare is important. Would you put a massive **chandelier** in a tiny home? You could, but you would not have room to move around! A big light fixture works alongside arrangements of large furniture. That puts the design in proportion to the size of a larger home. Scale is a difficult idea to master. The general rule is to vary the sizes and proportions of each object, and to link the objects to one another with color or texture.

This large, striking chair sits comfortably in the wide-open space it occupies. Its scale is in proportion to the grand landscape seen behind and around it. This chair would overwhelm a smaller space.

BALANCE

Balance in a room can be created with symmetry. It can be created by the furniture, artwork, or accessories. When planning your design scheme, begin by imagining your room as a **grid**. Ensure that objects, artwork, furniture, window treatments, and design details balance each other in color, shape, pattern, or scale.

LINING UP

It is also important to consider the lines of a room. Your eyes move around a room by following the lines of the walls, the furniture, or other items in the room. You can use lines to direct where people look when they enter a room. For example, a table can be a line that points to a particular feature in the room.

Symmetry, balance, and harmony in this space are provided by the lighting positioning and the vases.

Makers and Shakers

Zeynep Fadillioglu

In 2009, the first known woman to design the interior of a mosque balanced scale and proportion to create Istanbul's Sakirin Mosque. That woman was Zeynep Fadillioglu (born 1955), a designer from Turkey. Zeynep studied art history and design rather than **architecture**. The mosque is a great example of modern design combined with traditional Islamic art. It is a serene space with a beautiful chandelier. Fine, decorative metalwork covers the large windows, allowing plenty of light in.

THE MEASURE OF A ROOM

Interior designers never start decorating before they have studied a space. They also need an accurate floor plan. Without it, it is like playing a new board game without instructions. You just guess where the pieces go and hope for the best. Floor plans are the framework for design.

ONE WALL, TWO WALLS, THREE, AND FOUR

To measure a room, you need a tape measure, and a pen and paper. For accuracy, be sure to measure to the nearest quarter inch (0.5 cm). Draw a square on the paper to roughly match the room shape. Label the sides of the square 1 through 4. Match each measurement to the correct number on your sketch of the room. If you have an L-shaped room, you will have more walls to measure.

Today, most designers use software programs to design floor plans. This allows them to create and change the floor plans and room designs until they are happy with their design.

With your tape measure, start measuring the space, including:

- The length of the first wall along the baseboard from one corner of the room to another
- Repeat for the second, third, and fourth walls
- The height of each wall from floor to ceiling
- All the doorways and how far they are from the ends of the walls so that you can put them in the right place on your final plan
- The direction the door swings (in or out)
- All the room's windows, including the distance from the bottom of the window to the floor, and from the window to the corner of the wall (or to the next window or opening)
- Any permanent shelves or built-in desks or fireplaces, and their distance to the corner of the wall
- Where the electrical outlets, light switches, and any heating or air conditioning vents are located

This three-dimensional plan of a living room shows what it will look like when constructed.

Be a Maker!

To get the **dimensions** accurately represented on paper, early designers took all the measurements of a space and plotted them on a piece of graph paper. Technology now allows us to build three-dimensional spaces on computers. What new technological advances would you like to see in the future that you think will help interior designers?

MAKE IT!
A MODEL PLAN

Models not only look good, they have a purpose. After measuring a space, you can create a mini-replica and use it to help you find the focal point and build a design around it. You can work on your own or as a group—remember, makers are inspired by collaboration, so if you know someone you think you would work well with, why not create a team project?

1
- Measure your room and draw a diagram of the floor and each wall.
- Transfer the diagram of each section onto foam board or cardboard.
- Use a ruler and a craft knife to cut out each section. Add to your measurements an amount equal to the width of the board so your walls overlap at the edges for easy gluing.

2
- After you have cut out all the pieces use glue or tape to attach the walls to the floor.

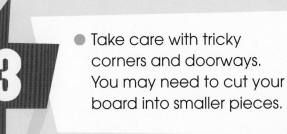

3 ● Take care with tricky corners and doorways. You may need to cut your board into smaller pieces.

4 ● Check the finished model. Are all the sides the right way around? Make sure none are upside down!

Make It Even Better!

Congratulations! You have a basic room model. Now go one step further. Start adding additional elements such as flooring, paint, and maybe even a little bit of the furniture. How will you apply what you have learned about creating a model to the next room you design? If you worked as part of a team, share your thoughts.

CONCLUSION

How did your model turn out? Does it help you visualize the room? Talk with your group about what you think you could do to improve it.

HARMONY IN SPACE

When we sing in harmony, it makes a beautiful sound. When a design is harmonious, it makes a beautiful space in which all the individual parts work together. Harmony can be achieved through repetition and rhythm. Repetition is the repeating of similar elements. Rhythm is the way your eyes move around the room. It should be a flowing movement. Your eyes should not be tripped up by any one item.

The blue, pale gray, brown, and orange colors used in this room design work well together to give the room a unified feel.

CREATING UNITY

Harmony and unity are important elements in design. Look at the room above. Imagine replacing the brown couch with a bright red couch. How would the couch affect the look of the room? Would the room still be harmonious and have unity?

SECRETS OF FENG SHUI

Feng shui (pronounced fung shway) is an ancient Chinese way of creating a harmonious space. It organizes spaces to increase positive energy in our environment. Everything has energy, even nonliving objects. Feng shui helps let that energy flow freely through your home. This cannot be accomplished overnight, but it might be worth considering in your designs.

USING FENG SHUI IN DESIGN

- Get rid of dark corners of negative energy by adding lighting.
- Put a water fountain or aquarium facing the front door to welcome positive energy into the space.
- Place sofas against solid walls with a clear view of the door.
- Use circular or oval coffee tables to allow energy to move around more easily.
- Declutter. In feng shui, nothing new flows into your life until you make room for it.

Makers and Shakers

Frank Lloyd Wright

Architect and interior designer Frank Lloyd Wright (1867–1959) added furniture, lighting, and decorative arts into the structure of his buildings. This was referred to as organic architecture. It allowed him to achieve a harmonious and unified interior. When Wright created a building, the decor, layout, and furniture were part of this maker's overall vision. Every element was connected.

The circular bands in Frank Lloyd Wright's Guggenheim Museum create a sense of flowing energy. The area feels open and spacious.

SPICE IT UP!

Place a white pillow on a black leather couch and you have **contrast**. Contrast is easy to see in black and white. You can also find contrast by putting splashes of color in a room. Put an orange cushion on a blue couch and you have contrast. The same is true when you place a soft cushion on a hard bench. They are strong opposites of each other.

WHAT IS CONTRAST?

Contrast is a design feature that can add visual interest. You can use colors, patterns, textures, or shapes to provide contrast. Hanging a round light fixture over a square table provides contrast. So does a smooth, wooden coffee table on a thick rug. What other contrasts can you think of?

Contrast and **variety** are often related in interior design. Both need to be used effectively. Not enough and the design looks dull. Too much and the design appears chaotic.

Black and white have been used in this room to contrast with each other. The result is an interesting space.

PLAYING WITH DESIGN

The Sims is a life **simulation** game that gives you the power to create and control people. It also lets you design homes and interiors. Games like this allow us to play with concepts such as contrast and variety. It makes it easy to see what works and what overloads a space. Is there too much contrast and variety or not enough?

This space is full of bold, bright, and contrasting colors. What effect does the design have on you?

Be a Maker!

Professional interior designers do not usually work for themselves: they are hired by clients. Designers need to match the overall design to the personality of the client. They sometimes make choices a client might not like. It is important to fix these small elements. Have a friend or family member pretend they are your client. Have them review your room design board. What do they like? What would they change? Is the clients' negative feedback valid? If not, explain why you disagree with it.

THE FINAL TOUCHES

Paint? Check. Focal point? Check. Furniture? Check. Accessories? Oh yeah, almost forgot about that! Accessories and one-of-a-kind touches change a basic design to an outstanding one. Final touches complete the vision. This is where your personality gets to shine. What would your bedroom design be without the poster of your favorite band or sports hero?

ARRANGING FINAL TOUCHES

- Change the display of your favorite pieces from time to time, rather than putting everything out at once. Avoid a feeling of clutter.
- Follow the rule of odd numbers. Arrange objects or pictures in groups of threes or fives. They are more appealing than sets of twos or fours.
- Vary heights, shapes, and textures to hold visual interest but keep one similar feature such as varied tins that are all metal, pillows that are all blue, or teddy bears that are all white.

SHOW PIECES

Designers often create new pieces of furniture or artwork specifically for a particular space. Old pieces of wooden furniture are given new life with a coat of funky paint. Some pieces are taken apart and rebuilt as something new. This is called **upcycling**.

The red leather chair takes center stage in this room design. Notice how it is positioned in front of the mirror and highlighted by the lamp to bring it into full focus.

Upcycling is a process in which old objects or fabrics are recycled to make a new product. It is not a new idea. Historically, everything in the home was reused. Old sheets were turned into rag rugs and dresses became quilts. Back then it was a matter of necessity. Today, upcycling is a design style that is also good for the environment.

This amazing armchair has been upcycled from a wooden packing crate!

Makers and Shakers

Elsie de Wolfe

Elsie de Wolfe (1865–1950) was living in a man's world when she became one of the first female interior designers in the early 1900s. Many people refer to her as the mother of modern interior design. Elsie was something of a rebel. She moved from a career on stage to practice her own version of design that was very different from the cluttered style of the time. Elsie promoted simple and airy designs, using mirrors and light colors of paints and fabrics. If you became a designer, what do you think your signature style would be?

MAKE IT!
UPCYCLE AWAY!

It is time! You have read through this makerspace book, and now you are ready to start a project of your own. Designing an entire room is a big task. Designing a one-of-a-kind piece of furniture that will fit into your design is more manageable. It is time to take what you have learned about color, texture, patterns, scale, lines, and unity, and put them to work by designing a custom piece of furniture that will fit well into your space. Remember—you can work as a team.

YOU WILL NEED
- A small, old table
- Sandpaper
- Large sheet of rough, thin paper, such as newspaper
- Pencil
- Scissors
- Sewing pins
- Fabric or paper with a pattern
- Water-based emulsion paint
- 1-inch (2.5-cm) paintbrush
- **Decoupage**
- White glue (optional)

- Sand down any rough wood and clean off any grime.
- Put the tabletop upside-down on a large piece of rough paper. Draw around it. Measure the depth of the tabletop, plus an extra half inch (1.5 cm). Draw a second line that same distance around the first, to create a template. Cut around this outer line.

1

2

- Carefully pin your template to the fabric or paper. Remember to keep it the right way up. Cut it out.
- Give the table a few coats of paint and leave it to dry.

● Coat the top, sides, and a bit of the underside of the table with decoupage (or white glue). Place your fabric or paper on the table. Smooth out any air bubbles or creases. Fold the edges neatly under the table. Press firmly so the edges stick to the table. Leave it to dry.

3

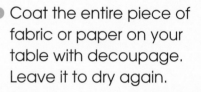

4

● Coat the entire piece of fabric or paper on your table with decoupage. Leave it to dry again.

CONCLUSION

Take a look at your upcycled table. Did it turn out the way you hoped? Did you encounter any problems? If you did, did you turn them into positives, in true maker style? How would you improve your design? Share your ideas with your team.

Make It Even Better!

Take a good look at your project. What decisions did you have to make during the design process to create this piece? What could you change to make it better? If you worked as a team, do you feel you have created a piece that you all love? How would you change it or improve it?

29

GLOSSARY

accessories Small pieces that make a room more visually appealing

architecture The practice of designing and constructing buildings

centuries A period of 100 years

chandelier A decorative hanging light with many branches or lightbulbs

chaotic In a state of complete confusion and disorder

clients People using the services of an interior designer or other professional

collaborative Produced or conducted by two or more people working together

commission An official assignment

composition The way in which the parts of something are put together or arranged

contrast The effect achieved by placing strikingly different objects, shapes, or colors close together

decoupage A glue, sealer, and finish used to attach fabric and paper to various surfaces

dimensions The measurements of something

elements The various parts that make up something

floral Relating to or using flowers

function The purpose of something

geometric Made with simple lines and shapes

grid A pattern of lines that cross each other to make squares

harmony A pleasing combination of things

interior designers People who decorate and furnish rooms in homes or offices

makerspace A do-it-yourself space where people gather to learn, create, and invent

neutral color A color such as black, white, gray, or brown

palette The range of colors used for a particular project

proportion The size of something in relation to something else

scale The relative size of things

simulation Something that is made to behave like something else, so that it can be studied

symmetry A situation in which two sides or halves of a room are the same or very close

texture The feel of something when it is touched or its visual appearance

unity The relationship of all the elements in a space and how they work together

upcycling Reusing discarded objects or fabric in an innovative way

upholstery The thickly padded fabric that is used to cover furniture such as armchairs and couches

variety A collection of different things

LEARNING MORE

BOOKS

Becker, Holly, and Joanna Copestick. *Decorate: 1,000 professional design ideas for every room in your home*. Chronicle Books, 2011.

Doorley, Scott, *and Scott Witthoft. Make Space: How to Set the Stage for Creative Collaboration*. Wiley, 2012.

Minecraft Books. *Minecraft: Book of House Design*. Blurb, 2015.

Quinton, Emily. *Maker Spaces*. Ryland Peters & Small, 2015.

WEBSITES

KidsThinkDesign is all about being creative in fashion, graphics, and, of course, interior design:
www.kidsthinkdesign.org/interiors/index.html

Discover more about home decor:
http://makezine.com/tag/home-decor-3

Try out the Discovery Kids "Room Maker" game:
http://discoverykids.com/games/room-maker

Check out this Lego-style apartment:
www.youtube.com/watch?v=juWaO5TJS00

Could you live in a tiny cube home?
www.youtube.com/watch?v=ZXtMpQk9lyw

INDEX